# WHAT IS
# CONTEMPORARY
# ART?

FROM THE COLLECTION OF THE MUSEUM OF MODERN ART, NEW YORK

# WHAT IS CONTEMPORARY ART?

## A Children's Guide

Jacky Klein and Suzy Klein

WITH 74 COLOUR ILLUSTRATIONS

Thames & Hudson

# CONTENTS

INTRODUCTION   06

A SPLASH OF COLOUR   08

LIGHT FANTASTIC   10

DRIPS, DOTS AND WAVES   12

WHAT'S IN A NAME?   14

FACE TO FACE   16

GOING ROUND IN CIRCLES   18

BIZARRE BEASTS   20

ALL THAT GLITTERS   22

LINE UP   24

GETTING DRESSED   26

SEEING DOUBLE   28

ALL WHITE   30

FLYING HIGH   32

MAKING AND BREAKING   34

LIFE SIZE   36

38 SPARKLES AND CHOCOLATE

40 ORIGINALS AND COPIES

42 BALANCING ACT

44 READ ALL ABOUT IT

46 BLACK HOLES AND MOON ROCKS

48 OVER AND OVER

50 THE ARTIST'S BODY

52 PLAYING GAMES

54 BEDTIME

56 ARTISTS' BIOGRAPHIES

60 GLOSSARY

61 WHERE TO FIND OUT MORE

61 WHERE TO SEE MORE

62 PICTURE CREDITS

63 INDEX

64 ABOUT THE AUTHORS

64 ACKNOWLEDGMENTS

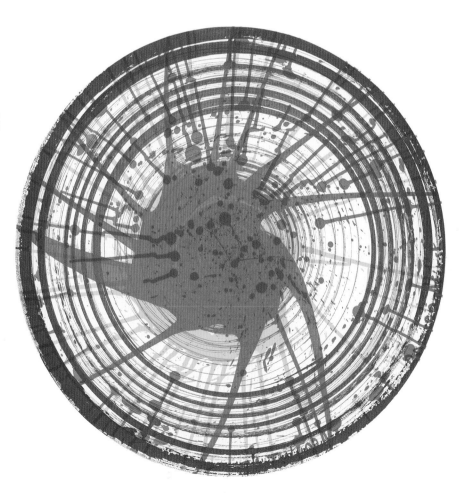

# INTRODUCTION

**WHAT DO YOU THINK CONTEMPORARY ART IS?**
**PAINTINGS AND DRAWINGS?**
**SCULPTURES AND PHOTOGRAPHS?**

When you visit a museum of contemporary art, you will see all of these things – but you will also find much more. That's because artists are constantly inventing new ways to make art. They still use paint, ink, marble and bronze, but since the 1960s they have also produced videos, put on performances and made installations.

Artists today love to experiment and break away from tradition. They often use the most unexpected materials, like elephant dung, crushed cars or chocolate. By transforming the things that we might think of as disposable and everyday, contemporary artists are always reinventing and re-imagining.

**WHAT IS CONTEMPORARY ART?** guides you through this exciting world.

Here, you will find artworks grouped together by theme, exploring the ideas and techniques shared by artists from across the globe. At the back of the book there are some helpful explanations of key art words – wherever you see the *asterisks*, just turn to the glossary. You will also find information on all of the artists in the book, and a list of useful websites and contemporary art museums showing where you can go next.

Today, more than ever, art is about asking questions and setting your own rules. It's as much about ideas and feelings as how an artwork looks. Contemporary artists want us to open our eyes and see the world differently. We invite you to get involved – by looking, exploring, enjoying and questioning.

**WHAT IS CONTEMPORARY ART?** Let's find out...

**INSPIRING**

This book includes artworks about games, outer space and bizarre beasts. It explores the building blocks of art, such as shapes, lines and colours, and it's full of art made from surprising materials such as electric light and empty eggshells. Take a look inside: which works do you find most inspiring?

# A SPLASH OF COLOUR

Yves Klein, *Anthropometry: Princess Helena*, 1961

**SOMETHING BLUE HAS SMEARED ITSELF ACROSS THIS PIECE OF PAPER. WHAT COULD IT HAVE BEEN?**

The artist Yves Klein was obsessed with just one colour: blue. He worked with a chemist to develop his own brand of paint, which he called International Klein Blue. It had a particularly bright and intense colour. He applied the paint to his pictures using rollers, sponges and even people! This work is part of a series in which Klein used naked female models as "living paintbrushes". The women were covered in blue paint and lay down on large sheets of paper, rolling around or dragging each other as directed by the artist. The body prints created by these *performances* made surprising shapes and patterns.

Olafur Eliasson, *The colour spectrum series*, 2005

## A WORLD OF COLOUR

Throughout history, colours have always had particular associations. Red can mean love or danger; blue often symbolises loyalty, wisdom or truth. Olive green is traditionally the colour of peace, while dark green is associated with greed and jealousy. Imagine your favourite colour: what does it make you think of, and how does it make you feel?

**Olafur Eliasson** likes to use the widest variety of colours he can find for his artworks. In the past he has created a giant orange indoor sun, made a real rainbow in a gallery, and dyed a river green. This block of *prints* shows us the complete range of colours the human eye can see, from deep violet at the top left corner to dark red at the bottom right. Eliasson wants us to think about how each one of us sees colours differently. Our understanding or perception of colour depends on our memories and emotions, even our family background and which country we come from. When you look at the grid, which green seems most like an apple to you, and which is most like broccoli? Do your friends choose the same colours as you?

# LIGHT FANTASTIC

Dan Flavin, *"monument" 1 for V. Tatlin*, 1964

**SOMETIMES SIMPLE, EVERYDAY MATERIALS CAN CREATE DAZZLING WORKS OF ART.**

This light sculpture was made by the artist Dan Flavin using fluorescent tubes that he attached to the wall. Flavin liked to work with the sort of lightbulbs he could find in any electrical shop. The bulbs offered him a new material for his art, and a fixed system of shapes and colours that he found he could adapt into countless different arrangements. This sculpture gives off a bright white light, but if you look closely, the wall around it also seems to shine. Can you spot the delicate halo all around the edge? What effect do you think this has on the artwork?

### FIVE SHAPES, TEN COLOURS

Dan Flavin used a very limited range of bulbs in his work, even though many more were available. He chose just five shapes (a circular bulb and four straight ones of varying lengths) and only ten colours (red, blue, green, pink, yellow, ultraviolet and four different shades of white).

This work by Bruce Nauman is like a poem written in light. Nauman makes letters out of glass neon tubes, which can be bent into any shape he wants. Neon is bright and eye-catching, and is often used to advertise places such as beauty salons or fast-food restaurants. But Nauman isn't trying to sell us a product. Instead, he uses flashing neon to create words that ask us to look deep inside ourselves. What do you desire, need or hope for?

Bruce Nauman, *Human/Need/Desire*, 1983

Jackson Pollock, *White Light*, 1954

# DRIPS, DOTS AND WAVES

## LOOK AT THIS EXPLOSIVE PAINTING BY THE ARTIST JACKSON POLLOCK.

Pollock was known as an *Abstract Expressionist*. He liked to express his feelings through colour and line rather than painting real or recognisable objects. Every part of this painting asks for your attention, all at once. Where do your eyes lead you?

### DRIPS AND SPLATTERS

Jackson Pollock dripped and threw paint onto his canvases, moving the colours around with trowels and knives instead of brushes. His technique became so famous he was known as "Jack the Dripper"!

Roy Lichtenstein, *Girl with Ball*, 1961

Bridget Riley uses a different technique in her optical or *Op art* paintings. She creates visual illusions, tricking your eyes into seeing movement and vibration when your brain knows that you are only looking at lines on a flat surface. Concentrate on this painting for a few seconds: can you see the lines begin to dance and wave?

Bridget Riley, *Current*, 1964

This might look like a picture from a magazine but it is a carefully constructed painting, inspired by an advert for a holiday resort. Roy Lichtenstein often copied the simple style and *primary colours* of the comic books he had loved as a child. Here, he paints the girl's skin using small dots, making her appear as if she has been printed in a newspaper or comic strip.

# WHAT'S IN A NAME?

## THESE ARTWORKS HAVE ONE THING IN COMMON: NONE OF THEM HAS A TITLE. WHY DO YOU THINK THAT IS?

This painting made with white crayon on grey paint is by Cy Twombly. It's known as one of his "Blackboard Paintings" because the scrawled lines look like chalk on a blackboard. Twombly lived in Rome in Italy, and his scribbles are similar to the graffiti on the city's monuments and walls. But it is impossible to identify any words here. Twombly deliberately made his painting mysterious rather than clear or readable, so that we can find our own meanings in it.

### HOW DID HE DO IT?

Twombly's painting is huge: the size of a small cinema screen. He couldn't easily reach the top of the canvas, so he invented a clever technique: he sat on the shoulders of his *studio assistant*, Nicola del Roscio, who shuttled back and forth along the canvas. This allowed Twombly to continue his long, unbroken lines.

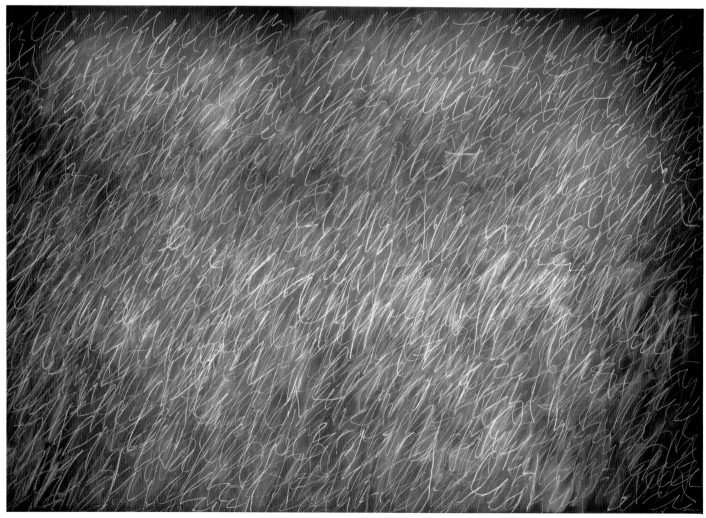

Cy Twombly, *Untitled*, 1970

14

"Random piling, loose stacking, hanging, give passing form to the material.... Chance is accepted...."

Robert Morris

What do these drooping parallel strips look like to you? Robert Morris's early sculptures were made of rigid materials, such as steel, but he switched to working with soft materials, such as felt, because he wanted to introduce movement and chance into his work. Here, the cut panels of felt hang from the gallery wall and sag in the middle. Gravity plays an important part in the shape of the artwork. Morris's soft sculptures could also be piled up or stacked on the floor, allowing the same piece to make different shapes. He didn't give titles to these sculptures because they can be moved and changed, so their meaning can change too.

Nam June Paik, *Untitled*, 1993

Nam June Paik was a composer and pioneer of *video art*. In this untitled sculpture, a piano without a pianist mechanically plays ragtime music. Two cameras record the piano's inner workings, relaying the images onto thirteen television screens. Two more monitors show the image of the composer John Cage, whose ideas strongly influenced Paik. This work was left untitled to allow its meaning to stay open-ended.

Robert Morris, *Untitled*, 1969

### UNTITLED ART

Some artists choose not to name their artworks because they don't want to tell us exactly what to think. Instead, they invite us to come up with our own ideas. Ask your friends what names they would give these three works and see how many different answers you get.

# FACE TO FACE

ARTISTS HAVE ALWAYS LIKED TO RECORD
THEIR OWN FACES IN *SELF-PORTRAITS*.
BUT THESE TWO AREN'T QUITE WHAT
THEY SEEM...

This photograph by Gillian Wearing (opposite) is called *Self Portrait at 17 Years Old*. It seems to be an ordinary picture taken in a photo booth. But look very closely around her eyes and you'll notice something strange: the artist is wearing a mask. Gillian Wearing was forty years old when she made this artwork, re-creating a snapshot originally taken when she was seventeen. Disguising her face and neck behind a rubbery mask, Wearing carefully copied every detail of the earlier photo, including her hairstyle, clothes and even the booth's orange curtain. Is this new self-portrait truthful or fictitious? Or is it somewhere in between?

Chuck Close, *Self-Portrait*, 1997

## HOW DID SHE DO IT?

Gillian Wearing worked with a team of hair, makeup and special-effects artists to create her mask and wig. It was a long and expensive process, as the mask alone cost around £10,000. Wearing then took lots of pictures to capture the perfect image. As she says, "there is an art to making things look real".

At first glance, this looks like a pixellated photograph but in fact it's a painting based on a photograph. It was made using a diagonal grid filled with circles, ovals and triangles. American artist Chuck Close is well known for his enormous paintings of faces. This self-portrait looks like the kind of digital image you might create in moments on a computer or mobile phone, but Close's artworks take many months to complete as he meticulously paints them by hand.

Opposite: Gillian Wearing, *Self Portrait at 17 Years Old*, 2003

# GOING ROUND IN CIRCLES

**CIRCLES CAN BE NATURAL OR MAN-MADE, ANCIENT OR MODERN, AND CAN SUGGEST STILLNESS OR MOVEMENT.**

The stones in this circle come from Kilkenny in Ireland. They were picked up by the artist Richard Long after he took a walk there. Long loves nature and is famous for turning his walks into art. Sometimes he leaves an almost unnoticeable trace in the countryside, such as some dusty footprints. At other times, he writes a poem, takes a photograph or makes a sculpture for an art gallery. This circle has a timeless simplicity, like the still, ancient stone circles found all over England and Ireland.

## UNIVERSAL SHAPES

Have you ever drawn a circle in the sand or dragged a stick across the forest floor? Richard Long also likes creating simple shapes in the landscape, from lines and crosses to circles and spirals. He has made circles while walking in many remote locations, from the Andes mountains in South America to the Sahara desert in Africa. Long uses the materials he finds on each walk – including slate, wood or pine needles – to make natural shapes that echo the art of our prehistoric ancestors.

Richard Long, *Kilkenny Circle*, 1984

> "I think circles have belonged in some way or other to all people at all times.... For me, that is part of their emotional power...."
>
> Richard Long

**Damien Hirst** has made hundreds of paintings of coloured spots and spinning discs. He is fascinated by objects that go round in circles – whether it's the earth rotating or an old-fashioned vinyl record playing on a turntable. For the *print* below, he put a metal plate onto a specially made "spin machine" in his studio. As the machine whizzed around, Hirst scratched into the plate with needles, screwdrivers and other sharp tools. He then added coloured inks into the scratched grooves and pressed the metal plate onto paper to make his explosive, whirling circle.

Atsuko Tanaka, *Untitled*, 1964

**19**

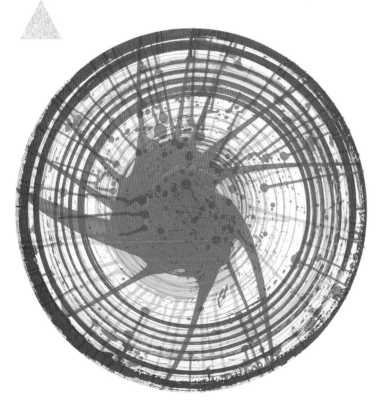

Damien Hirst, *Round* from *In a Spin, the Action of the World on Things*, Volume 1, 2002

What would inspire you to make a circular artwork? The inspiration for this painting by the Japanese artist Atsuko Tanaka came from an earlier sculpture she had made called *Electric Dress*. Tanaka was captivated by electricity and technology, and her dress was made from two hundred multicoloured flashing lightbulbs. She spent much of the rest of her life responding to her wearable sculpture by producing artworks almost entirely from lines and circles. The trailing lines and circles-within-circles in this painting almost look like electrical wires and lightbulbs.

# BIZARRE BEASTS

## TAKE A LOOK AT THESE STRANGE CREATURES. WHAT DO YOU THINK THEY COULD BE?

Nicolas Lampert's hybrid beast is part animal, part machine. His chameleon on a tank is one of a series of fantasy photographs that also includes a stag fused with a train and a praying mantis combined with a crane. Lampert pairs natural and mechanical forms to show the uncanny similarities between them. Here, both the chameleon and the tank are armour-plated, slow and predatory.

### MACHINE ANIMALS

Nicolas Lampert selects images from his own library of photocopies, then cuts and pastes them together by hand to make his machine–animal *collages*. He wants his images to look like they might be "a relic from the past, a lost scientific manual, or...a design for the future." Lampert loves animals and his art is a reaction to the destructive impact of both humans and machines on nature.

Nicolas Lampert, *Very Slow, Very Tired*, 2006

Have you ever seen one of these before? It's unlikely – because Joan Fontcuberta and Pere Formiguera have dreamed up another imaginary creature. They have photographically manipulated images to create animals that might be mistaken for specimens from a natural history museum. They call this beast *Alopex Stultus*, which translates as stupid wolf or fox, and they imagine it having the ability to camouflage itself as a shrub!

"The heart [of my work]... remains the questioning of photographic truth. Be careful, be critical, doubt.... This would be my advice."

Joan Fontcuberta

Joan Fontcuberta and Pere Formiguera, *Alopex Stultus*, 1985–88

# ALL THAT GLITTERS

## FROM ANCIENT TIMES TO OUR OWN, GOLD HAS BEEN ONE OF THE MOST ATTRACTIVE MATERIALS FOR ARTISTS.

This solid marble cube, weighing 1363 kilograms or 3000 pounds, is covered in gold that has been beaten into thin sheets known as gold leaf. It was made by James Lee Byars, whose artworks were shaped by a quest for perfection. Byars had an interest in Eastern religion and philosophy, and *The Table of Perfect* is intended to be shown in the centre of an empty room, like an altarpiece or holy shrine.

### THE ART OF GOLD

Where have you come across real gold? It's one of the rarest, most valuable materials on earth, usually reserved for jewellery and coins. It has also been used in religious art, from ancient Egyptian death masks to paintings of Christian saints and sculptures of Hindu gods. For artists today, it continues to symbolise perfection and divine beauty.

James Lee Byars, *The Table of Perfect*, 1989

Agnes Martin's painting *Friendship* is also covered in gold leaf. Martin is known for her delicate artworks featuring lines and grids, and here she has scored a geometric pattern into the surface of the gold. But her mathematical design is not intended to be rigid, and the shimmering painting is softened by the slight crookedness of her hand-cut lines. Martin wanted her artworks to reflect something personal, an inner emotional world. Her use of gold here suggests something precious and spiritual, like the very best friendships.

Agnes Martin, *Friendship*, 1963

The Spanish designer Martín Azúa has made a very useful artwork that you can carry around in your pocket. His portable house was created from a light, thin material with gold on one side and silver on the other. The golden side protects you from the cold, while the silver shields you from high temperatures. Azúa's shelter is so ingenious that it can be inflated using sunlight or simply the warmth of your own body. Azúa has used gold because it is both beautiful and practical. Do you think his house is a piece of art, design or architecture?

Martín Azúa, *Basic House*, 1999

### IN THE ARTIST'S OWN WORDS

Martín Azúa's gold-and-silver house was designed as a way to break free from material possessions and as an experiment in simple living. As he says, the house represents "A life on the move without material ties. Having everything without having scarcely anything."

# LINE UP

## DO YOU THINK THESE COLOURFUL LINES ARE LEAPING UP OR FLOWING DOWN?

To make this painting, the artist Morris Louis leaned the canvas against a wall and poured down streams of colour. He made sure the lines didn't smudge or blur into each other, but he was famously secretive about his painting technique and nobody knows quite how he did it. Louis left a lot of his canvas bare on purpose, so that the bright colours really jump out. It's the white space, as much as the lines, that make this painting so dramatic.

### THE "UNFURLEDS"

Louis made more than one hundred line paintings like this. They were huge – so big that it was impossible for him to completely unfurl the canvases in his dining room, which doubled as his studio. At the time, there weren't many art galleries big enough for them either, so only two were seen in public during the artist's lifetime. Louis called these paintings the "Unfurleds".

Morris Louis, *Beta Lambda*, 1961

The Spanish artist Eduardo Chillida also played with the relationship between lines and the space around them. In this drawing, he used black ink, which he applied to paper with a brush to create a group of chunky lines. Chillida is best known for his massive sculptures made from iron, steel, wood or granite, and the black lines here are similar to the thick interlocking shapes he used in his sculpture. Chillida loved to experiment with solid shapes and empty voids. As he said, "my whole work is a journey of discovery in space". The power of this drawing comes from the interplay between the "positive" space of the black lines and the "negative" space of the blank paper.

Eduardo Chillida, *Untitled*, 1966

Daniel Buren, *White Acrylic Painting on White and Anthracite Grey Striped Fabric*, 1966

Daniel Buren started making striped artworks in 1966. Almost all of his work features vertical lines of exactly the same width: 8.7 centimetres, or about as wide as an adult's hand. This painting on white-and-grey-striped cloth sits directly on the gallery floor. But Buren wants his distinctive lines to appear all over the place, not just in art galleries. He has planted striped rows of tulips, designed striped sails for boats, and even put his stripes on the outside of famous buildings, such as the Palais Royal in Paris. What's the most unusual thing you could imagine covering with stripes?

# GETTING DRESSED

## SOMEBODY HAS HUNG A SUIT ON THE WALL OF A GALLERY. WHY ISN'T IT AT HOME IN THE WARDROBE?

Joseph Beuys based this artwork on one of his own suits – but it wasn't meant to be worn. Its arms and legs are too long, it doesn't have any buttons, and it's made of felt, which is too stiff and itchy to wear. Beuys repeatedly used certain materials, such as felt and fat, because they had special associations with his past. He often told a story about when he was a fighter pilot in the Second World War and his plane crashed in Russia. He was rescued by tribesmen who covered his injured body in felt and fat to protect and comfort him. So for Beuys, felt was not just a sculptural material but also one full of personal memories.

### MULTIPLES

This is one of a hundred identical suits that Beuys made, in what is known as a *multiple*. Beuys made many multiples, including photographs, films and postcards. He wanted his artworks to be seen by as many people as possible and not just by the privileged few of the *art world*.

Joseph Beuys, *Felt Suit*, 1970

The artist Vito Acconci has taken another item of clothing out of the bedroom, this time from the underwear drawer. His gigantic bra can be placed in many different positions: on the floor, the wall, as a room divider and even hanging from the ceiling. The canvas-lined bra cups light up and are so large that you can sit inside them, where you'll hear a recording of someone breathing and you might catch the sound of distant voices or music. Acconci's piece of *installation art* invites the viewer to climb in and get involved. If you sat inside his bra, how would it make you feel?

Vito Acconci, *Adjustable Wall Bra*, 1990–91

# SEEING DOUBLE

## CLAES OLDENBURG'S DOUBLE CHEESEBURGER SEEMS GOOD ENOUGH TO EAT – BUT LOOK TWICE!

These juicy burgers might appear to be real, but they're made of thick cloth covered in hard painted plaster. They were created by Claes Oldenburg, who loves to make soft things in hard materials, and hard things in soft materials. Oldenburg is a *Pop artist* who is inspired by popular and commercial culture. Here, he celebrates America's favourite food with two burgers at nearly double their normal size. Does this doubling make them more or less appealing?

### REMAKING THE EVERYDAY

Oldenburg has made lots of sculptures based on real objects, including lipsticks and tubes of toothpaste. He often experiments with size and materials, once even sticking a giant melting ice cream made of steel on top of a German shopping centre. Rather than copying everyday things exactly, he transforms and re-imagines them.

Claes Oldenburg, *Two Cheeseburgers, with Everything (Dual Hamburgers)*, 1962

Felix Gonzalez-Torres chose another everyday item to double up. He took two matching battery-operated clocks and started them at exactly the same time. No two batteries are identical, however, so one of the clocks will slow down first and fall out of time with the other. Gonzalez-Torres made this work when he found out that his close friend Ross was seriously ill. He knew that, like the clocks, he and Ross would eventually fall out of synch. His clocks make us think about the strong bonds that exist between people who love each other, and about how the seconds and minutes of all our lives pass by.

Felix Gonzalez-Torres, *"Untitled" (Perfect Lovers)*, 1991

Judith Joy Ross, *The Stewart Sisters, H.F. Grebey Junior High School, Hazleton, Pennsylvania*, 1992

This portrait might make you do a double-take: it's a photograph of identical twins. Judith Joy Ross took the picture as part of a project she carried out at her old school in Pennsylvania in the United States. Going back there reminded her of her own childhood, and made her think about how we all change as we grow up. These two sisters may look alike, but there are already many differences between them. How many can you spot?

"When I look at somebody I think about their past and what their future could be, as well as what I'm seeing right now."

Judith Joy Ross

# ALL WHITE

## WITH ALL THE COLOURS OF THE RAINBOW TO CHOOSE FROM, WHY DO SOME ARTISTS PREFER TO STICK TO PLAIN WHITE?

Marcel Broodthaers took a table and a wall cabinet, painted them white and piled them high with eggs. He was fascinated by *Surrealist art* in which unlikely images, objects and materials were mixed together with surprising results. In this artwork, Broodthaers paired fragile white eggs with solid, antique-looking white furniture. The eggs he used are just empty shells that he described as "without content other than the air". He used white to suggest a similar kind of blankness, a lack of meaning. Try filling these eggshells with your own ideas: what story would the artwork tell?

Marcel Broodthaers, *White Cabinet and White Table*, 1965

### ON DISPLAY

Broodthaers made lots of artworks about museums and how they exhibit their treasures. This cabinet and table are things you might find at home, but Broodthaers chose them because they are also a bit like a museum display. The cabinet hangs on the wall as if it were a frame for a priceless painting, while the table sits on the floor like a pedestal or plinth for a sculpture.

Piero Manzoni, *Achrome*, 1962

Robert Ryman made this white-on-white
painting using twelve sheets of a heavy, cream-
coloured paper called Classico. He stuck these
to the wall in a grid using masking tape, which
he placed along the edges of each piece of paper.
He then painted a white off-centre square onto
the joined-up sheets. Once the paint was dry,
he peeled the tape off, leaving behind a ghostly
trace of small unpainted rectangles and lines.

Piero Manzoni chose white to make artworks
that were as neutral as possible. He wanted to
eliminate any outside ideas or references so that
his art was about nothing but itself. He made
white works using many different materials,
including clay, bread rolls, cotton padding and
rabbit skin. This furry picture was created using
white fibreglass wool that Manzoni shaped into
hair-like tufts. It is one of a series of works called
"Achrome", which was a made-up word. "Chrom"
is the Ancient Greek word for colour and "a"
means without, so these works are not so much
white as without colour.

Robert Ryman, *Classico 5*, 1968

Andreas Gursky, *Bahrain I*, 2005

# FLYING HIGH

## THIS PHOTOGRAPH WAS TAKEN FROM A HELICOPTER, HIGH IN THE AIR. WHAT DO YOU THINK THAT SNAKING BLACK LINE ON THE GROUND COULD BE?

This large aerial image, taken by Andreas Gursky, shows the looping tracks of the Formula 1 racing circuit in the desert of Bahrain in the Middle East. Gursky often takes pictures from high up because he likes to show us patterns and shapes that cannot be seen at ground level. He views the modern world as a place of advanced technology and vast scale where people are dwarfed by their environment. The cars on this track are tiny in relation to the sprawling asphalt landscape. Look very closely: can you find them?

This *screenprint* was based on an image from a newspaper. Using a stencil and a fabric screen, Gerhard Richter applied pink and green ink to cardboard. He made the colours not quite line up so that the three aeroplanes look blurred as they speed by. Richter was interested in jets because as a child he lived through the Second World War and his birthplace, Dresden in Germany, was badly bombed.

33

Gerhard Richter, *Flugzeug II (Airplane II)*, 1966

# MAKING AND BREAKING

## SOMETIMES DESTRUCTIVE OR VIOLENT ACTIONS CAN RESULT IN NEW KINDS OF ART.

This painting by Niki de Saint Phalle is an *assemblage*, an artwork made by putting together or assembling lots of different things collected by the artist. Can you spot the metal seat, shoe and toy gun? The work is from a series known as the "Shooting Paintings", in which Saint Phalle hid plastic bags filled with paint behind the wooden surface of the picture. She, her friends, or members of the public then shot at the paintings with a gun or rifle, bursting the bags and releasing streams of paint. Saint Phalle said she was aiming and firing at a society dominated by men. Her "Shooting Paintings" were acts of both creation and aggression.

34

### BIRTH AND DEATH

Niki de Saint Phalle found an original way of bringing painting to life. By incorporating dramatic action into the making of her artworks, she created paintings that were also spectacular *performances*. As she said, "It was an amazing feeling shooting at a painting and watching it transform itself into a new being. It was not only EXCITING...but TRAGIC – as though we were witnessing a birth and a death at the same moment."

Niki de Saint Phalle, *Shooting Painting American Embassy*, 1961

Lucio Fontana has taken a sharp blade and with a single stroke sliced through this unpainted canvas. His action might seem like an attack on painting itself, but Fontana saw it as creative rather than destructive. His slashed painting was an attempt to transform a flat, *two-dimensional* surface into a *three-dimensional* object. Do you think this artwork is a painting, a sculpture – or both?

"Many people have thought that I was trying to destroy. But that is untrue. I have made and not destroyed."

Lucio Fontana

Lucio Fontana, *Spatial Concept: Expectations*, 1960

# LIFE SIZE

**THIS SCULPTURE SHOWS
A MAN STANDING IN THE
CORNER WITH HIS HANDS
BEHIND HIS BACK. WHAT DO
YOU THINK HE IS UP TO?**

The artist Martin Kippenberger
made a replica of himself, *cast* it in
aluminium and dressed it in his own jeans,
shirt and shoes. His sculpture is called
*Martin, Into the Corner, You Should Be
Ashamed of Yourself*. Kippenberger made
it after a journalist wrote something
particularly nasty about his work. The
artist's response was to create a life-size
sculpture of himself facing the wall,
pretending he had been told off like a
naughty child. Kippenberger was well-
known for being a prankster who loved to
poke fun at the *art world*. Who or what
do you think he is trying to provoke with
this artwork?

Martin Kippenberger, *Martin, Into the Corner,
You Should Be Ashamed of Yourself*, 1992

In this sculpture, George Segal sat a life-size plaster figure on an old bus seat that he had found in a scrapyard. Segal made dozens of life-size sculptures which he placed in real environments, using *found objects* such as street signs and park benches. He was inspired to make this artwork after meeting a grumpy driver on the night bus going home.

Michelangelo Pistoletto, *Man with Yellow Pants*, 1964

George Segal, *The Bus Driver*, 1962

### HOW DID HE DO IT?

Segal's brother-in-law was the model for this work. He was wrapped head-to-toe in bandages soaked in plaster and had to sit very still. He breathed through his nose using two tiny airholes until the plaster dried hard. Segal then cut off the bandages, sticking them back together again to make a hollow shell in the shape of a person.

What's going on here? This man seems to be leaning against the wall of an art museum. In fact, he is a life-size image painted onto the surface of a mirror. Michelangelo Pistoletto's artwork often surprises people in the gallery when they catch sight of themselves reflected in the mirror and realize that the man is not real. It's an *interactive* work that changes as people move in and out of view. The gallery visitor is as much a part of the painting as the life-size man.

# SPARKLES AND CHOCOLATE

## WHAT'S THE MOST UNUSUAL THING YOU COULD USE TO MAKE A PAINTING OR SCULPTURE?

This painting of a man with an afro hairstyle (opposite) features lots of surprising materials, including sparkly glitter, map pins and magazine cutouts of famous black people. Look carefully and you'll also notice three brown balls: one on the man's necklace and two on the floor. These are made of elephant dung, which the artist, Chris Ofili, got from a zoo. Dung has become his trademark and makes his work instantly recognisable.

John Chamberlain, *Essex*, 1960

39

John Chamberlain used scrap metal to make his sculptures. He especially loved old cars and he cut, crushed and twisted their metal parts into colourful shapes. You might expect a used car to end up in a rubbish dump, but Chamberlain shows us that secondhand materials can have new life, beauty and meaning even after their original job is done.

Dieter Roth, *Basel on the Rhine*, 1969

Does this brown swirly picture look hard or soft? It's made from two very different materials: tough steel and gooey chocolate. The artist Dieter Roth often worked with food. He once made a sculpture with forty suitcases packed full of cheese. He liked making artworks that rotted and changed over time. This picture is slowly decomposing: the white blotches are the fats in the chocolate that have risen to the surface in the forty years since it was made. What do you think it might look like in another forty years' time?

### ANYTHING GOES!

There's no limit to the unexpected and thought-provoking materials some contemporary artists choose. Just take a look through this book: can you find empty eggshells, fluorescent lightbulbs and model railway trains?

# ORIGINALS AND COPIES

## SOMETIMES A REPLICA CAN MAKE US LOOK EVEN MORE CLOSELY AT THE ORIGINAL THAT INSPIRED IT.

The small painting on the wall, on the far left, was made by the artist Francis Alÿs. Alÿs lives in Mexico, where brightly coloured, hand-painted adverts are common, and he invited two local sign-painters to copy and enlarge his original. He encouraged them to change and improve his painting as they wished. What alterations have they made? And how does the presence of the two copies in Alÿs's *installation* change how we look at the original?

### CHINESE WHISPERS

Francis Alÿs is a *conceptual artist* who is interested in ideas and concepts as much as in the final appearance of his artworks. This installation comes from a larger series called the "Sign Painting Project", which resulted in more than one hundred paintings by Alÿs and his team of sign-painters. Alÿs compared the series to an artistic game of Chinese whispers, where the original image changes in small ways each time it is repainted by another artist.

40

Francis Alÿs, *Untitled*, 1994

"[I wanted] to create a challenge for your eyes. I wanted your eyes to open wider."

Vija Celmins

Vija Celmins is also interested in imitation and replicas. In this work, called *To Fix the Image in Memory*, she displays eleven stones that she collected while on a walk in northern New Mexico, in America. Alongside the original stones are identical copies of each that Celmins made in bronze. Can you match up all of the pairs? Celmins wanted her casts exactly to resemble the stones she had found, encouraging us to look closely and intensely. Which stones do you think are real here, and which are artificial?

### HOW DID SHE DO IT?

Celmins picks up many stones on her walks, but she keeps only those with the most interesting surfaces and patterns. She kept these stones in the boot of her car for a long time, occasionally taking them out to admire them. Eventually she decided to make copies of them, *casting* the stones in bronze. It then took her five years to paint them carefully by hand.

41

Vija Celmins, *To Fix the Image in Memory*, 1977–82

# BALANCING ACT

## CONTEMPORARY ARTISTS CAN MAKE US GASP WITH THEIR GRAVITY-DEFYING FEATS.

This steel sculpture by the American artist **Barnett Newman** is around seven-and-a-half metres high, or about as tall as a two-storey building. It was made in the 1960s during a time of political unrest and race riots in the United States. Newman created his artwork using a pair of ancient Egyptian forms: a pyramid and an obelisk, turned upside-down and broken. Take a look at the tiny point where the two parts meet: the work seems to defy gravity. In fact, there is a steel pole hidden inside that keeps it upright. Why do you think Newman decided to shear off the top of the monument?

### MONUMENTAL

Ancient obelisks were massive columns that stood outside temples as impressive reminders of death and the afterlife. Newman wanted his broken obelisk to suggest both sadness and joy. As he said, "I hope that I have transformed its tragic content into a glimpse of the sublime."

Barnett Newman, *Broken Obelisk*, 1963–69

Peter Fischli and David Weiss, *The Way Things Go*, 1987

When Peter Fischli and David Weiss worked together, amazing things happened. Their film *The Way Things Go* shows a series of finely balanced chain reactions in which everyday objects fall, rotate and explode, propelling each other forward. The transfer of energy between balloons and cups, oil drums and mattresses makes for an inventive relay race. The film stills above come from a sequence in which a candle lights a fuse wire, releasing a tyre which rolls across ramps and seesaws before toppling a ladder.

## HOW DID THEY DO IT?

Fischli and Weiss experimented for a whole year to perfect their ingenious film. In the same way that other artists make sketches, they first shot a three-minute test film of key sequences to make sure they worked. The final thirty-minute film relied on a precise balance of chemical and physical reactions.

43

This sculpture was created by the artist Richard Serra using four large metal plates. What do you think is holding them up? Together they weigh a massive 909 kilograms, or a ton, but they are freestanding and are not attached either to each other or to the floor. Serra has been fascinated by industrial materials ever since he worked in a steel mill to pay his way through university. His propped-up sculpture might seem dangerous, as if the heavy lead slabs could topple over, but they are kept in perfect balance by the force of gravity.

Richard Serra, *One Ton Prop (House of Cards)*, 1969 (REFABRICATED 1986)

# READ ALL ABOUT IT

THESE THREE ARTISTS USE LANGUAGE TO GIVE THEIR WORK ITS POWER AND MEANING. WHAT EFFECT DO THEIR WORDS HAVE ON YOU?

Korean artist Do Ho Suh often explores the idea of home and our feelings of homesickness when we're away. "Welcome" is a word we encounter at a boundary, for instance when entering a new country or stepping over the threshold of a home. Suh lives between Seoul, New York and London, and his doormat is an expression of how it feels to move between different places and cultures.

Do Ho Suh, *Doormat: Welcome* (and detail), 1998

## ALL IN THE DETAIL

Suh's doormat is made up of hundreds of identical tiny rubber figures with their arms raised. Suh often uses miniatures like this in his work. He is fascinated by how we as individuals relate to each other and to the society we live in.

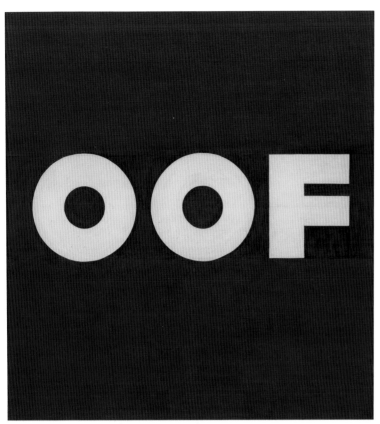

Ed Ruscha, *OOF*, 1962 (REWORKED 1963)

OOF! Ed Ruscha's large painting, as tall as a grown-up, spells out a noise of the kind you might see in a comic book punch-up. Many of Ruscha's paintings feature words on simple backgrounds. Just like adverts, they immediately grab our attention. Ruscha studied *graphic design* and typesetting alongside art. His capital letters here are in bold type rather than scrawly handwriting, making them direct and forceful. But his word appears alone, more like a sign or logo than part of a story. What sounds and actions does the painting conjure up for you?

This warning sign by Antoni Muntadas offers a bold message about our relationship with art and the wider world: that to perceive or truly understand something, we must get involved. Muntadas is a *multimedia artist* who works with photography, *video*, *installation* and *urban interventions*. This sticker comes from a long-term project of printed works written in different languages. The *series* is all about words, their translation and their interpretation.

## WORDPLAY

Over the last hundred years, words have become an ever-more important element in art. Artists love things that are a bit unclear, and words allow them to play with double meanings. By using language in their artworks, they can provoke and instruct us, make statements and tell stories.

45

Antoni Muntadas, *On Translation: Warning*, 1999–PRESENT

Chris Burden, *Medusa's Head*, 1990

# BLACK HOLES AND MOON ROCKS

## TAKE A LOOK AT THIS GIANT METEOR-LIKE SCULPTURE BY CHRIS BURDEN.

Called *Medusa's Head*, it is named after the mythical Greek creature Medusa who had snakes for hair and turned everyone who looked at her into stone. Instead of snakes, Chris Burden has used model railway tracks and trains, crisscrossing a mass of steel, rock and cement. What does his otherworldly sculpture make you think of?

### SPACE

Some artists make works that look like they're from outer space, while others are interested in darkness and infinity. As Lee Bontecou says, "I like space that never stops.... Black is like that. Holes and boxes mean secrets and shelter."

Anna Maria Maiolino, *Buraco Preto (Black Hole)* from the series "Os Buracos/Desenhos Objetos" (Holes/Drawing Objects), 1974

Anna Maria Maiolino has created a mysterious black hole by the simplest of means: layers of black paper that she has torn in circles and mounted on top of each other. Maiolino loves to cut and fold paper, and here she turns the flat, *two-dimensional* sheets into a *three-dimensional* sculpture, creating a sense of dark, infinite space.

Lee Bontecou is fascinated by outer space and many of her wall-mounted constructions feature voids and black holes. This one was made at the dawn of the space age in the 1960s, soon after the first satellite had orbited the earth. Bontecou used unusual materials in this sculpture, including leather and soot, as well as old canvas conveyor belts. These *found objects* came from the laundry below her flat in New York.

Lee Bontecou, *Untitled*, 1961

# OVER AND OVER

Donald Judd, *Untitled (Stack)*, 1967

ARTISTS HAVE ALWAYS
TRIED TO BE ORIGINAL, SO
WHY DO THESE TWO LOVE
TO REPEAT THEMSELVES?

Donald Judd's sculptures were based
on simple forms that he used time and
again. This stack of twelve identical green
boxes hangs on the wall like a series of
paintings but it also projects outwards
into the gallery. Each box is exactly
9 inches or 22.9 centimetres high, and
the artist gave instructions that the
space between them also had to be
22.9 centimetres. Judd was interested
in how the placing or *installation*
of a sculpture affects the way we feel
about it. For him, repetition was a
way of drawing our attention away
from individual boxes and towards the
experience of the artwork as a whole.

## MINIMAL ART

Donald Judd was a *Minimalist* artist
who liked basic, pared-down shapes. Most
of his art was made using sequences of
rectangles and cubes that either sat on
the floor or ran up or across the wall.
He wanted the individual parts of his
sculptures to be identical, so he had them
produced in industrial workshops rather
than making them by hand.

## REPEAT AND REWORK

When Andy Warhol found a subject that excited him, he came back to it again and again. He captured the soup can in countless paintings, prints, watercolours and drawings. He focused on subjects that he loved, whether it was soup or Coca-Cola, banknotes or film stars. What are your favourite things and how would you make an artwork inspired by them?

Take a close look at these thirty-two paintings of Campbell's soup cans: can you spot the differences between them? At first glance they appear to be identical, but Andy Warhol made each one with a different label, showing all the varieties of Campbell's soup that were then available. Every can here is the same size and shape because Warhol wanted to highlight how similar and even monotonous they looked. His originality lay in his repetition of images from everyday life, and his transformation of cheap consumer goods into works of art.

"I used to drink [Campbell's soup]. I used to have the same lunch every day, for twenty years...the same thing over and over again."

Andy Warhol

Andy Warhol, *Campbell's Soup Cans*, 1962

# THE ARTIST'S BODY

## CONTEMPORARY ARTISTS OFTEN USE THEIR OWN BODIES AS THE INSPIRATION FOR THEIR ART.

**What kind of body do you see here?** John Coplans pointed his camera at his own knobbly knees and wrinkled hands to show us a very honest portrait of his ageing body. He started making black-and-white photographs after he turned sixty, to document himself in old age. His images encourage us to think about what makes a body beautiful or ugly.

John Coplans, *Self Portrait*, 1985

Have you ever put your hand into paint, pressed it onto paper, and made a handprint? Janine Antoni used her eyelashes in the same way. She put on lots of mascara, brought her face up close to the paper and started blinking. Her beautiful *abstract* picture was made with the most delicate part of her body. What creative ways can you think of to use your body in an artwork?

51

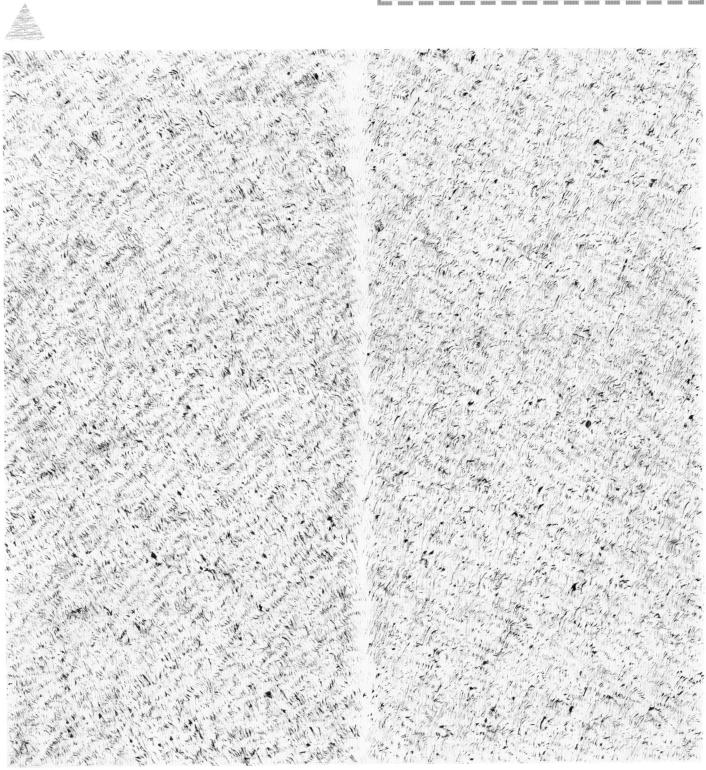

Janine Antoni, *Butterfly Kisses*, 1996–99

# PLAYING GAMES

JEFF KOONS HAS SUSPENDED THREE BASKETBALLS IN A GLASS CASE HALF FILLED WITH WATER. WHAT'S HE PLAYING AT?

This is one of a series of tanks Jeff Koons made for an exhibition he called "Equilibrium", meaning balance. Exactly half of each ball is under water, and Koons worked with several scientists to achieve this effect. He has taken a popular, ordinary object – a basketball – and turned it into something extraordinary and worthy of our attention in a museum.

Jeff Koons, *Three Ball 50/50 Tank (Two Dr. J. Silver Series, One Wilson Supershot)*, 1985

Blinky Palermo, *Flipper*, 1970

This pair of *abstract* prints was created by the German artist **Blinky Palermo.** Called *Flipper*, it takes its name from the German word for pinball, which Palermo loved to play. The red, white and blue geometric pattern copies the design on the pinball machine at his local café. In the left-hand panel, the blue lines have been removed. What effect does this have on the artwork as a whole?

### RULE-BREAKING

What's your favourite game? The artists here were all inspired by a sport or a hobby. In each case they have either changed the game or broken its rules to create their artworks.

Gabriel Orozco,
*Horses Running Endlessly*, 1995

Gabriel Orozco has made an art out of re-imagining games, inventing a billiard table without pockets and a ping-pong game featuring a lily pond. Here, he has created his own version of chess. His board is four times the normal size and uses four colours instead of just black and white. Orozco has also left out all of the pieces except for the knights, or horses, so the usual rules of the game have disappeared. His chessboard is no longer a competitive battlefield but a landscape of the imagination.

# BEDTIME

## WE ALL LOVE TO CLIMB INTO A COMFY BED AT THE END OF THE DAY. WHY DOESN'T THIS ONE LOOK VERY INVITING?

Rachel Whiteread's bed is unmade: it's just a mattress. If you look closely, especially around the edges, you'll notice too that it's made of something hard – in this case, plaster. Whiteread made her mattress shortly after her father died, as a reminder that bed is not just a place of sleep but also sometimes of illness. Her sculpture transforms an everyday object from the home into a monument to sadness and loss.

### NOOKS AND CRANNIES

Rachel Whiteread has made mattresses using many materials, including plaster, resin and rubber. She has also *cast* other things from around the home, such as baths and dressing tables. Whiteread is fascinated both by the objects themselves and the spaces around them. By casting unusual places such as the undersides of chairs or the insides of wardrobes, she invites us to pay attention to the overlooked and unexplored. Take a look around your bedroom: how well do you know all of its nooks and crannies?

54

Rachel Whiteread, *Untitled (Mattress)*, 1991

Louise Bourgeois used her *autobiography*, or life story, in her art. Her work centred on emotions and obsessions, and often focused on her own family. Bourgeois's parents had a stormy relationship that deeply affected her, and she saw the bedroom as a place where family dramas were played out. The tiny figure here, dwarfed by a giant bed, might seem lonely or vulnerable. But this bedroom could also be a place of imagination and dreams. What thoughts and feelings does Bourgeois's bed inspire in you?

## CHILDHOOD MAGIC

Louise Bourgeois made this *print* when she was in her eighties. Even then, the memories of her youth remained strong. As she said, "My childhood has never lost its magic, it has never lost its mystery, and it has never lost its drama. All my work… all my subjects, have found their inspiration in my childhood."

Louise Bourgeois, *Bed #1, state I*, 1997

# ARTISTS' BIOGRAPHIES

**VITO ACCONCI** (American, born 1940)

**Famous for:** Sculpture, video and performance art, especially an early performance piece in which he followed strangers through the streets of New York

**Fascinating fact:** Acconci's father made bathrobes for a living.

**FRANCIS ALŸS** (Belgian, born 1959)

**Famous for:** Conceptual and performance art, which often involves walking

**Fascinating fact:** Alÿs once got five hundred volunteers to move an entire sand dune by just a few centimetres, in the desert outside Lima in Peru.

**JANINE ANTONI** (Bahamian, born 1964)

**Famous for:** Performances that involve her own body, including sculpting portraits of herself from chocolate and soap

**Fascinating fact:** Antoni spent her childhood in Freeport in the Bahamas, where she loved to make sandcastles on the beach.

**MARTÍN AZÚA** (Spanish, born 1965)

**Famous for:** Ingenious environmental designs

**Fascinating fact:** Azúa designed the medals for the 2003 World Swimming Championships, including a transparent, bubble-filled swimming medal.

**JOSEPH BEUYS** (German, 1921–86)

**Famous for:** Installations using fat and felt

**Fascinating fact:** Beuys almost always wore the same outfit: jeans, a felt hat and a fishing vest.

**LEE BONTECOU** (American, born 1931)

**Famous for:** Wall-mounted sculptures made from welded steel frames and found objects

**Fascinating fact:** Bontecou's father and uncle invented the world's first aluminium canoe.

**LOUISE BOURGEOIS** (American, born France, 1911–2010)

**Famous for:** Sculptures and installations, especially her giant spider sculptures

**Fascinating fact:** Bourgeois loved cooking, and one of her favourite foods was oxtail stew.

**MARCEL BROODTHAERS** (Belgian, 1924–76)

**Famous for:** Artworks made using eggs and mussel shells

**Fascinating fact:** Broodthaers once interviewed a cat about its views on contemporary art.

**CHRIS BURDEN** (American, born 1946)

**Famous for:** Performance art, especially his early work that placed him in extreme physical danger

**Fascinating fact:** Burden created a performance piece while at university which involved him spending five days and nights inside a gym locker.

**DANIEL BUREN** (French, born 1938)

**Famous for:** Striped artworks

**Fascinating fact:** Buren has designed striped scarves for the French fashion house Hermès.

**JAMES LEE BYARS** (American, 1932–97)

**Famous for:** Mysterious performances, installations and objects made from gold, glass and stone

**Fascinating fact:** Byars often dressed in a gold suit and top hat.

**VIJA CELMINS** (American, born Latvia 1938)

**Famous for:** Detailed paintings and drawings of the night sky, the sea and spiders' webs

**Fascinating fact:** When Celmins was young, her mother drew a picture of a pansy for her. Today, Celmins surrounds herself with the flowers to remind her of her mother.

**JOHN CHAMBERLAIN** (American, 1927–2011)

**Famous for:** Sculptures made from crushed cars

**Fascinating fact:** Chamberlain trained as a hairdresser and makeup artist before becoming a sculptor.

**EDUARDO CHILLIDA** (Spanish, 1924–2002)

**Famous for:** Large abstract sculptures made from steel or iron

**Fascinating fact:** As a young man, Chillida was the goalkeeper for the Spanish football team Real Sociedad, but had to retire because of a knee injury.

**CHUCK CLOSE** (American, born 1940)

**Famous for:** Large-scale portraits based on photographs

**Fascinating fact:** Close has a condition known as "face blindness", or prosopagnosia, where he finds it impossible to recognise people's faces.

**JOHN COPLANS** (British, 1920–2003)

**Famous for:** Black-and-white photographs of his own naked body

**Fascinating fact:** Coplans was a fighter pilot during the Second World War.

**OLAFUR ELIASSON** (Danish, born 1967)

**Famous for:** Artworks that re-create natural phenomena such as rainbows, ice, steam and waterfalls

**Fascinating fact:** As a teenager, Eliasson was in a breakdancing crew that won the Scandinavian championships two years in a row.

**PETER FISCHLI AND DAVID WEISS**
(Swiss, born 1952 and Swiss, 1946–2012)

**Famous for:** Adapting everyday objects to create witty artworks; known especially for their film *The Way Things Go*

**Fascinating fact:** The artists' first collaboration was a series of photographs called *Wurstserie (Sausage Series)*, featuring small scenes made with various kinds of sausages and meat.

**DAN FLAVIN** (American, 1933–96)

**Famous for:** Fluorescent light sculptures and installations

**Fascinating fact:** As a young man, Flavin was a guard and lift operator at The Museum of Modern Art, New York.

**LUCIO FONTANA** (Italian, 1899–1968)

**Famous for:** Slashed or punctured canvases

**Fascinating fact:** Fontana would often spend days or even weeks looking at a painting before deciding where to make a cut in its surface.

**JOAN FONTCUBERTA** (Spanish, born 1955)

**Famous for:** Photographs that question the nature of truth and illusion, especially his images of fictitious hybrid animals

**Fascinating fact:** Fontcuberta has no formal training as an artist and started his career in advertising.

**PERE FORMIGUERA** (Spanish, born 1952)

**Famous for:** Photographs of his family and friends

**Fascinating fact:** One of Formiguera's projects involved taking photographs of more than thirty people once a month for ten years, to see how they changed as they grew older.

**FELIX GONZALEZ-TORRES** (American, born Cuba, 1957–96)

**Famous for:** Sculptures made from piles of sweets

**Fascinating fact:** Gonzalez-Torres's father bought him his first set of watercolours when he was six years old.

**ANDREAS GURSKY** (German, born 1955)

**Famous for:** Large-scale, highly detailed photographs of supermarkets, stock exchanges and blocks of flats

**Fascinating fact:** Gursky's parents were both professional photographers and taught him the basics of photography when he was a young boy.

**DAMIEN HIRST** (British, born 1965)

**Famous for:** Sculptures featuring animals in glass tanks suspended in formaldehyde, especially his pickled tiger shark

**Fascinating fact:** Hirst is a compulsive collector – alongside a huge number of contemporary artworks, he has also bought totem poles, skulls, a cow with six legs and hundreds of fake Picasso paintings.

**DONALD JUDD** (American, 1928–94)

**Famous for:** Minimalist sculptures in metal, plywood, concrete and plexiglass, often in the shape of cubes or rectangles

**Fascinating fact:** Judd was obsessed by cacti and every time he moved house his desert plants came with him.

**MARTIN KIPPENBERGER** (German, 1953–97)

**Famous for:** A rebellious attitude and provocative artworks, particularly his self-portraits

**Fascinating fact:** Kippenberger's favourite food was pasta and he included it in lots of his paintings and drawings.

**YVES KLEIN** (French, 1928–62)

**Famous for:** Paintings made with his trademark blue paint called International Klein Blue

**Fascinating fact:** Klein had a blackbelt in judo and wrote a book about the martial art. After spending two years in Japan, he even set up his own judo club in Paris.

**JEFF KOONS** (American, born 1955)

**Famous for:** Highly polished steel sculptures of inflatable rabbits and balloon dogs

**Fascinating fact:** Koons worked as a banker on Wall Street in New York while he was establishing himself as an artist.

**NICOLAS LAMPERT** (American, born 1969)

**Famous for:** Collages that combine animals with machines

**Fascinating fact:** Lampert has made a series of artworks called "Meatscapes", featuring enormous pieces of meat placed in a variety of locations, from the pyramids in Egypt to the American Wild West.

**ROY LICHTENSTEIN** (American, 1923–97)

**Famous for:** Pop art paintings that reproduce comic book images using small dots of paint

**Fascinating fact:** Lichtenstein was a gifted musician – he played piano, clarinet and jazz flute, and started a school jazz band.

**RICHARD LONG** (British, born 1945)

**Famous for:** Turning his walks into art by leaving traces in the landscape or creating texts and sculptures

**Fascinating fact:** Long's headmistress let him paint and draw during assembly, when the other students had to sing hymns.

**MORRIS LOUIS** (American, 1912–62)

**Famous for:** Colourful paintings made by pouring paint down the canvas

**Fascinating fact:** Louis was very secretive about his work – not even his wife was allowed into his studio.

**ANNA MARIA MAIOLINO** (Brazilian, born Italy 1942)

**Famous for:** Sculptures made from unfired clay, and drawings in which she cuts, tears and stitches together paper

**Fascinating fact:** Maiolino is the youngest of ten brothers and sisters.

**PIERO MANZONI** (Italian, 1933–63)

**Famous for:** Creating ninety sealed tin cans filled with his own poo

**Fascinating fact:** For one of his exhibitions, Manzoni made some hard-boiled eggs, "signed" them with his thumbprint, and then gave them away for the audience to eat.

**AGNES MARTIN** (American, born Canada, 1912–2004)

**Famous for:** Subtle abstract paintings featuring grids and lines

**Fascinating fact:** Martin lived alone all of her adult life and avoided modern means of communication. Her home had no television, radio, music or telephone.

**ROBERT MORRIS** (American, born 1931)

**Famous for:** Grey plywood structures and sculptures made from felt

**Fascinating fact:** Morris has choreographed several pieces of contemporary dance and was married to a dancer and choreographer.

**ANTONI MUNTADAS** (Spanish, born 1942)

**Famous for:** Multimedia works and public art installations that focus on social and political issues

**Fascinating fact:** Whenever Muntadas starts a new art project he goes to his favourite place to be inspired: the picture collection of the New York Public Library.

**BRUCE NAUMAN** (American, born 1941)

**Famous for:** Performances, videos, installations and neon sculptures, especially his spiral neon which reads: "The true artist helps the world by revealing mystic truths"

**Fascinating fact:** Nauman lives and works on a ranch in New Mexico in America, where he raises horses and cattle.

**BARNETT NEWMAN** (American, 1905–70)

**Famous for:** Large paintings featuring lines of colour that he called "zips"

**Fascinating fact:** Newman once ran for election as the mayor of New York City.

**CHRIS OFILI** (British, born 1968)

**Famous for:** Using elephant dung in his art

**Fascinating fact:** Ofili once owned a lime-green car with a horn that made a bellowing sound like an elephant.

**CLAES OLDENBURG** (American, born Sweden 1929)

**Famous for:** Giant sculptures of everyday objects such as lipsticks, apple cores and washing pegs

**Fascinating fact:** Oldenburg moved from Sweden to America when he was six years old. He couldn't speak English, so he and his younger brother created a made-up world complete with detailed maps, newspapers, adverts and film posters.

**GABRIEL OROZCO** (Mexican, born 1962)

**Famous for:** Inventive sculptures, including a black-and-white-patterned human skull and a Citroën car with its middle section cut out

**Fascinating fact:** Orozco is a constant traveller and divides his time between Paris, New York and Mexico City. He uses his plane tickets and foreign banknotes in many of his artworks.

**NAM JUNE PAIK** (Korean-American, 1932–2006)

**Famous for:** Large-scale television-screen and video installations

**Fascinating fact:** Paik studied music at the University of Tokyo in Japan.

**BLINKY PALERMO** (German, 1943–77)

**Famous for:** Colourful paintings, often made using strips of fabric

**Fascinating fact:** Palermo's real name was Peter Schwarze. He was nicknamed Blinky Palermo because he looked like a mafia gangster of the same name.

**MICHELANGELO PISTOLETTO** (Italian, born 1933)

**Famous for:** Paintings made directly onto the surfaces of mirrors

**Fascinating fact:** When he was fourteen years old, Pistoletto began an apprenticeship in his father's art restoration business in Turin in Italy.

**JACKSON POLLOCK** (American, 1912–56)

**Famous for:** Paintings made by dripping, throwing and splashing paint onto the canvas

**Fascinating fact:** Pollock's life and work were turned into a Hollywood film starring the actor Ed Harris as the painter.

**GERHARD RICHTER** (German, born 1932)

**Famous for:** Paintings made in a variety of styles, including multicoloured grids and blurry paintings based on photographs

**Fascinating fact:** At the age of sixteen, Richter left school and trained as an apprentice set-painter in a theatre.

**BRIDGET RILEY** (British, born 1931)

**Famous for:** Op art paintings in which abstract shapes and patterns seem to move and have depth

**Fascinating fact:** Riley once took shelter in the doorway of a London art gallery to avoid a rainstorm. The owner, Victor Musgrave, invited her in and looked at her artworks – the following year, his gallery presented her first solo exhibition.

**JUDITH JOY ROSS** (American, born 1946)

**Famous for:** Small black-and-white portrait photographs

**Fascinating fact:** Ross once received a phone call notifying her that she had won a £16,000 award for her work. She had never heard of the prize, but she gratefully accepted the money.

**DIETER ROTH** (German-Swiss, 1930–88)

**Famous for:** Artworks made from rotting food including cheese, chocolate, yoghurt and bananas

**Fascinating fact:** Roth once collaborated with the artist Richard Hamilton on an exhibition for dogs, where all the pictures were hung at dog-eye level.

**ED RUSCHA** (American, born 1937)

**Famous for:** Paintings of petrol stations and mountains, which often incorporate words and phrases

**Fascinating fact:** Ruscha has made art from a wide range of materials including bolognese sauce, baked beans, daffodils and grass stains.

**ROBERT RYMAN** (American, born 1930)

**Famous for:** White paintings on square canvases

**Fascinating fact:** Ryman came to New York as a young man to pursue a career in jazz. While in the city, he got a job as a security guard at The Museum of Modern Art.

**NIKI DE SAINT PHALLE** (French, 1930–2002)

**Famous for:** Paintings in which she shot at the canvas with a gun or rifle, and brightly coloured, larger-than-life sculptures of women

**Fascinating fact:** During her twenties, Saint Phalle modelled for *Vogue*, *Life* and other magazines.

**GEORGE SEGAL** (American, 1924–2000)

**Famous for:** Life-size sculptures of people made from unpainted plaster

**Fascinating fact:** Segal grew up on a poultry farm in New Jersey in America. After he got married, he bought his own chicken farm where he held annual picnics for his friends from the New York art world.

**RICHARD SERRA** (American, born 1939)

**Famous for:** Giant public sculptures made from rolled steel

**Fascinating fact:** One of Serra's most treasured memories is of his fourth birthday, when he was taken to watch the launch of a vast new tanker at the shipyard where his father worked.

**DO HO SUH** (Korean, born 1962)

**Famous for:** Delicate fabric sculptures of houses including his childhood home in Seoul, Korea, and his flat in New York

**Fascinating fact:** Suh has always had a passion for studying fish and wanted to be a marine biologist before he became an artist.

**ATSUKO TANAKA** (Japanese, 1932–2005)

**Famous for:** Creating an electric dress made from two hundred lightbulbs painted red, blue, green and yellow

**Fascinating fact:** Tanaka had four older sisters and four older brothers.

**CY TWOMBLY** (American, 1928–2011)

**Famous for:** Large-scale paintings featuring writing, scrawls and graffiti

**Fascinating fact:** Twombly once worked in the army as a cryptographer, deciphering secret codes.

**ANDY WARHOL** (American, 1928–87)

**Famous for:** Paintings and prints of celebrities and soup cans

**Fascinating fact:** Warhol had a studio in New York called "The Factory" which became a famous meeting place for artists and socialites, musicians and performers.

**GILLIAN WEARING** (British, born 1963)

**Famous for:** A series of photographs in which people held up handwritten signs revealing their private thoughts

**Fascinating fact:** Wearing loves roller coasters and took her partner, the artist Michael Landy, to a theme park on their first date.

**RACHEL WHITEREAD** (British, born 1963)

**Famous for:** Sculptures cast from household objects and unusual spaces; known especially for casting the inside of an entire house using concrete

**Fascinating fact:** Whiteread loves to go beachcombing with her two sons on the banks of the River Thames in London, where they have collected old pipes, lead balls, ammunition and bones.

# GLOSSARY

## *Abstract art*

Art based on colour and shapes, often geometrical ones. Abstract art does not show clearly recognisable people, places or objects.

## *Abstract Expressionism*

A style developed by American painters in the 1940s and 1950s. Their art was abstract, and they expressed their thoughts and feelings through colours and shapes rather than by painting people or things.

## *Art world*

The art world is made up of all the people who make, buy, sell, write about and exhibit works of art.

## *Assemblage*

An artwork in which the artist has gathered together or assembled a collection of everyday objects. It might be a two-dimensional collage or a three-dimensional sculpture.

## *Autobiography*

An autobiography tells the story of someone's own life in a book, play, film or artwork.

## *Casting*

Pouring liquid material, such as plaster or molten bronze, into a mould. When the liquid sets solid, it is removed to make an artwork.

## *Collage*

Art made by sticking pieces of paper, photographs, newspaper or fabric onto a surface. Contemporary artists also use computers to create digital collages by cutting and pasting images together.

## *Conceptual art*

Art in which concepts or ideas are just as important as the materials used or the final look of the artwork. Conceptual artists ask questions about what art is, and they often produce performances, photographs or installations rather than traditional paintings or sculptures.

## *Found objects*

Natural or man-made objects found by an artist and used to inspire or create their artworks.

## *Graphic design*

The art of combining text and images to deliver a message, for example on websites, or in magazines, books and adverts.

## *Installation*

The act of hanging, placing or installing works of art. "Installation" can also be used as a shorthand for "installation art".

## *Installation art*

An artwork usually designed for one particular place and sometimes just for a short period of time. Installation art is often made of many separate parts, and can take up an entire room or gallery.

## *Interactive artwork*

A work of art in which you, the viewer, are encouraged to participate. An interactive artwork is only really made complete when you become involved.

## *Materials*

The physical things needed to make a work of art, such as canvas, plaster, marble or paint.

## *Medium / media*

A medium is the material or substance an artist uses to make their work, such as paint or video. Media is the plural of medium.

## *Minimalism / Minimal art*

A type of pared-back abstract art that first appeared in the 1960s. Minimal art uses simple, geometric shapes such as squares and rectangles, and is often created from modern industrial materials.

## *Multimedia artist*

An artist who likes to make artworks from many different media or materials, rather than only working in one medium such as painting or sculpture.

## *Multiple*

An artwork made in a number of identical copies by the artist him- or herself. The number produced is usually limited and the copies together are known as an edition.

## *Op art*

An art style developed in the 1960s that created optical effects in painting. Op artists use shapes, lines and patterns to produce the effect of vibration or depth in their artworks.

## *Painting*

The art of applying paint to a surface to create a picture. A painting usually features paint on canvas, but in contemporary art it can be any artwork that uses paint as the main material, applied to any surface.

## *Performance art*

Art that involves a series of actions usually performed by the artist. The performance can be spontaneous or carefully planned, carried out in private or seen by many people in a public place. This type of art is often documented in photographs, films and videos.

## *Photography*

The art of taking and printing photographs. Photographs can be black-and-white or colour, and can be produced using a film camera or a digital camera.

## *Pop art*

An art that draws its imagery, style and inspiration from popular culture and mass media, including adverts, comic strips and consumer goods.

## *Primary colours*

The three primary colours are red, yellow and blue. They are "primary" because they can be mixed together in different amounts to create every other colour.

## *Print*

An image created by pressing ink onto a sheet of paper or any other surface. The ink can be transferred from a metal plate, a stone, a block of wood, a fabric screen or a smooth material called linoleum. Photographic prints are made using light-sensitive materials.

## *Screenprint*

A kind of print made using a fabric screen that is stretched tightly over a frame. Areas of the screen that are not going to be printed are blocked out by a stencil. A roller or squeegee is then used to push the ink through the open parts of the fabric onto a sheet of paper.

## *Sculpture*

A three-dimensional artwork usually made by chiselling, modelling or carving a material such as bronze or wood. Sculptures can also include everyday or found objects.

## *Self-portrait*

A portrait of the artist by the artist. Self-portraits can be drawn, painted, sculpted or photographed.

## *Series*

A number of artworks by an artist that together form a group. Works in a series will usually be made in the same materials as each other, or share similar imagery.

## *Studio assistant*

Someone who assists in a studio, the place where an artist works. An assistant can help to prepare materials, produce artworks, organise exhibitions or carry out duties such as paying bills or ordering supplies.

## *Surrealism / Surrealist art*

A style of art that began in the 1920s in which familiar objects are presented in an unexpected or surprising way. The Surrealists were particularly interested in dreams and the unconscious mind.

## *Three-dimensional*

A three-dimensional artwork is one that projects out into space or has depth, such as a sculpture. The three dimensions refer to the length, width and depth of the object.

## *Two-dimensional*

A two-dimensional artwork is one made using a flat surface, for instance a painting or photograph. The two dimensions refer to the length and width of the artwork.

## *Urban intervention*

An artwork, performance or installation in a city that uses parts of the urban environment such as walls, statues, buildings or parks. Many urban interventions are inspired by the artist's political or environmental concerns.

## *Video art*

Art made using video or television. Video art can take many forms, including recordings shown in a gallery, installations that include television monitors, or live broadcast events.

## WHERE TO FIND OUT MORE

**The Art Story**
www.theartstory.org
**Artcyclopedia**
www.artcyclopedia.com
**Dia Art Foundation, New York**
www.diacenter.org
**Guggenheim Museum, New York**
www.guggenheim.org
**The Museum of Modern Art, New York**
www.moma.org
**Oxford Art Online**
www.oxfordartonline.com
**Tate, UK**
www.tate.org.uk

## WHERE TO SEE MORE

All of the artworks featured in this book are in the collection of The Museum of Modern Art, New York. Below is a selection of some other great museums with permanent collections of international contemporary art:

### UK
**Tate**, London, Liverpool and St Ives, England
**Scottish National Gallery of Modern Art**, Edinburgh, Scotland

### REST OF EUROPE
**Arken Museum of Modern Art**, Copenhagen, Denmark
**Centre Georges Pompidou**, Paris, France
**Fondation Beyeler**, Basel, Switzerland
**Irish Museum of Modern Art**, Dublin, Ireland
**Kunsthalle Hamburg**, Germany
**Kunstmuseum Basel**, Switzerland
**Kunstmuseum Liechtenstein**, Vaduz, Liechtenstein
**Louisiana Museum of Modern Art**, Humlebaek, Denmark
**Moderna Museet**, Stockholm, Sweden
**Moscow Museum of Modern Art**, Russia
**Musée d'Art Moderne de la Ville de Paris**, France
**Museo Nacional Centro de Arte Reina Sofía**, Madrid, Spain
**Museu d'Arte Contemporani de Barcelona**, Spain
**Pinakothek der Moderne**, Munich, Germany
**Staatliche Museen zu Berlin** - Neue National Galerie and Hamburger Bahnhof, Museum für Gegenwart, Berlin, Germany
**Staatsgalerie Stuttgart**, Germany
**Stedelijk Museum**, Amsterdam, The Netherlands
**Stedelijk Museum voor Actuele Kunst (SMAK)**, Ghent, Belgium

### NORTH AMERICA
**Art Gallery of Ontario**, Toronto, Canada
**Art Institute of Chicago**, Illinois
**Dia Art Foundation**, New York
**Menil Collection**, Houston, Texas
**Museum of Contemporary Art**, Los Angeles, California
**National Gallery of Art**, Washington
**National Gallery of Canada**, Ottawa, Canada
**Philadelphia Museum of Art**, Pennsylvania
**San Francisco Museum of Modern Art**, California
**Solomon R. Guggenheim Museum**, New York
**Walker Art Center**, Minneapolis, Minnesota
**Whitney Museum of American Art**, New York

### REST OF THE WORLD
**Gallery of Modern Art**, Queensland, Australia
**Museum of Contemporary Art**, São Paulo University, Brazil
**Museum of Contemporary Art**, Sydney, Australia
**The National Museum of Modern Art**, Tokyo, Japan
**São Paulo Museum of Art**, Brazil
**Tehran Museum of Contemporary Art**, Iran
**Tel Aviv Museum of Art**, Israel

# PICTURE CREDITS

All works are from the collection of The Museum of Modern Art, New York. Dimensions are given in centimetres, height before width before depth.

**p.1** Atsuko Tanaka, *Untitled*, 1964
Synthetic polymer paint on canvas, 333.4 x 225.4
John G. Powers Fund. Photo John Wronn. © 2012 Ryoji Ito

**pp. 2–3** Francis Alÿs, *Untitled*, 1994
Oil on canvas and synthetic polymer paint on sheet metal, three panels, small panel by Francis Alÿs 31.8 x 25.4, medium panel by Emilio Rivera 91.4 x 71.4, large panel by Juan Garcia 120 x 91.4
Gift of Eileen and Peter Norton. Courtesy David Zwirner, New York

**p.4** John Chamberlain, *Essex*, 1960
Automobile parts and other metal, 274.3 x 203.2 x 109.2
Gift of Mr and Mrs Robert C. Scull and purchase. Photo John Wronn. © ARS, NY and DACS, London 2012

**p.5** Damien Hirst, *Round* from *In a Spin, the Action of the World on Things*, Volume 1, 2002
One from a portfolio of twenty-three etching, aquatint and drypoints, sheet 91.2 x 69.9
The Associates Fund. Photo Thomas Griesel. © Hirst Holdings Limited and Damien Hirst. All rights reserved, DACS 2012

**p.8** Yves Klein, *Anthropometry: Princess Helena*, 1961
Oil on paper on wood, 198 x 128.2
Gift of Mr and Mrs Arthur Wiesenberger. Photo Mali Olatunji. © ADAGP, Paris and DACS, London 2012

**p.9** Olafur Eliasson, *The colour spectrum series*, 2005
Series of forty-eight photogravures, composition (each) 26.8 x 46; sheet (each) 34.5 x 46. Publisher Niels Borch Jensen Verlag and Galerie, Berlin. Printer Niels Borch Jensen Værksted for Koppertryk, Copenhagen. Edition 18
Riva Castleman Endowment Fund. Photo John Wronn. © Olafur Eliasson

**p.10** Dan Flavin, *"monument" 1 for V. Tatlin*, 1964
Fluorescent lights and metal fixtures, 243.8 x 58.7 x 10.8
Gift of UBS. © ARS, NY and DACS, London 2012

**p.11** Bruce Nauman, *Human/Need/Desire*, 1983
Neon tubing and wire with glass tubing suspension frames, 239.8 x 179 x 65.4
Gift of Emily and Jerry Spiegel. © ARS, NY and DACS, London 2012

**p.12** Jackson Pollock, *White Light*, 1954
Oil, enamel and aluminium paint on canvas, 122.4 x 96.9
The Sidney and Harriet Janis Collection. Photo Paige Knight. © The Pollock-Krasner Foundation, ARS, NY and DACS, London 2012

**p.13 left** Roy Lichtenstein, *Girl with Ball*, 1961
Oil on canvas, 153 x 91.9
Gift of Philip Johnson. Photo Kate Keller. © The Estate of Roy Lichtenstein / DACS 2012

**p.13 right** Bridget Riley, *Current*, 1964
Synthetic polymer paint on composition board, 148.1 x 149.3
Philip Johnson Fund. © Bridget Riley 2012. All rights reserved. Courtesy Karsten Schubert, London

**p.14** Cy Twombly, *Untitled*, 1970
Oil-based house paint and crayon on canvas, 405 x 640.3
Acquired through the Lillie P. Bliss Bequest and The Sidney and Harriet Janis Collection (both by exchange). © Cy Twombly

**p.15 left** Robert Morris, *Untitled*, 1969
Felt, 459.2 x 184.1 x 2.5
The Gilman Foundation Fund. © ARS, NY and DACS, London 2012

**p. 15 right** Nam June Paik, *Untitled*, 1993
Player piano, fifteen televisions, two cameras, two laser disc players, one electric light and light bulb, and wires, overall approximately 254 x 266.7 x 121.9, including laser disc player and lamp
Bernhill Fund, Gerald S. Elliot Fund, gift of Margot Paul Ernst, and purchase. © 2012 Estate of Nam June Paik

**p. 16** Gillian Wearing, *Self Portrait at 17 Years Old*, 2003
Framed chromogenic colour print, 115.5 x 92
Acquired through the generosity of The Contemporary Arts Council of The Museum of Modern Art. Photo Thomas Griesel. Courtesy Maureen Paley, London

**p. 17** Chuck Close, *Self-Portrait*, 1997
Oil on canvas, 259.1 x 213.4
Gift of Agnes Gund, Jo Carole and Ronald S. Lauder, Donald L. Bryant, Jr, Leon Black, Michael and Judy Ovitz, Anna Marie and Robert F. Shapiro, Leila and Melville Straus, Doris and Donald Fisher, and purchase. Photo Paige Knight. © Chuck Close. Courtesy The Pace Gallery, New York

**p. 18** Richard Long, *Kilkenny Circle*, 1984
Stones, 270 diameter
Gift of the Dannheisser Foundation. Photo Jonathan Muzikar. © Richard Long. All Rights Reserved, DACS 2012

**p. 19 left** Damien Hirst, *Round* from *In a Spin, the Action of the World on Things*, Volume 1, 2002
One from a portfolio of twenty-three etching, aquatint and drypoints, sheet 91.2 x 69.9
The Associates Fund. Photo Thomas Griesel. © Hirst Holdings Limited and Damien Hirst. All rights reserved, DACS 2012

**p. 19 right** Atsuko Tanaka, *Untitled*, 1964
Synthetic polymer paint on canvas, 333.4 x 225.4
John G. Powers Fund. Photo John Wronn. © 2012 Ryoji Ito

**p. 20** Nicolas Lampert, *Very Slow, Very Tired*, 2006
Digital print, composition (irregular) 78.7 x 139.7; sheet 111.8 x 159.4. Publisher Nicolas Lampert, Milwaukee, Wisconsin. Printer Prime Digital Media, New Berlin, Wisconsin. Edition unlimited, in varying scales
Fund for the Twenty-First Century. Photo Thomas Griesel. © Nicolas Lampert 2012

**p. 21** Joan Fontcuberta and Pere Formiguera, *Alopex Stultus*, 1985–88
One from a series of gelatin silver prints and ink with watercolour on paper, overall 42.7 x 37.8
Lois and Bruce Zenkel Fund. Photo Thomas Griesel. © DACS 2012

**p. 22** James Lee Byars, *The Table of Perfect*, 1989
Gold leaf on white marble, 99.7 x 99.7 x 99.7
Committee on Painting and Sculpture Funds. © The Estate of James Lee Byars

**p. 23 left** Martín Azúa, *Basic House*, 1999
Polyester, 200 x 200 x 200
Gift of Martín Azúa. Photo Daniel Riera

**p. 23 right** Agnes Martin, *Friendship*, 1963
Incised gold leaf and gesso on canvas, 190.5 x 190.5
Fractional and promised gift of Celeste and Armand P. Bartos. © 2012 Agnes Martin / DACS

**p. 24** Morris Louis, *Beta Lambda*, 1961
Synthetic polymer paint on canvas, 262.6 x 407
Gift of Mrs Abner Brenner. © 1961 Morris Louis

**p. 25 left** Daniel Buren, *White Acrylic Painting on White and Anthracite Grey Striped Fabric*, 1966
Synthetic polymer paint on striped cotton fabric, 228 x 197
Nina and Gordon Bunshaft Bequest and the Philip L. Goodwin Collection Funds (both by exchange). Photo John Wronn. © ADAGP, Paris and DACS, London 2012

**p. 25 right** Eduardo Chillida, *Untitled*, 1966

Ink on paper, 100.1 x 70.2
The Joan and Lester Avnet Collection. Photo Jonathan Muzikar. © Zabalaga-Leku, DACS, London 2012

**p. 26** Joseph Beuys, *Felt Suit*, 1970
Multiple of felt, overall 177.5 x 71.5 x 13.5 (irregular). Publisher Galerie René Block, Berlin. Fabricator unknown. Edition 100
The Associates Fund. © DACS 2012

**p. 27** Vito Acconci, *Adjustable Wall Bra*, 1990–91
Plaster, steel, canvas, light, lightbulbs and audio equipment, overall installation dimensions variable, 424.1 x 530.8 x 416.5
Sid R. Bass Fund and purchase. Courtesy Acconci Studio

**p. 28** Claes Oldenburg, *Two Cheeseburgers, with Everything (Dual Hamburgers)*, 1962
Burlap soaked in plaster, painted with enamel, 17.8 x 37.5 x 21.8
Philip Johnson Fund. Courtesy the Oldenburg van Bruggen Studio. © 1962 Claes Oldenburg

**p. 29 above** Felix Gonzalez-Torres, *"Untitled" (Perfect Lovers)*, 1991
Clocks, paint on wall, overall 35.6 x 71.2 x 7
Gift of the Dannheisser Foundation. © The Felix Gonzalez-Torres Foundation. Courtesy Andrea Rosen Gallery, New York

**p. 29 below** Judith Joy Ross, *The Stewart Sisters, H.F. Grebey Junior High School, Hazleton, Pennsylvania*, 1992
Gelatin silver printing-out-paper print, 24.8 x 19.5
Gift of Patricia Lawrence. © Judith Joy Ross. Courtesy Pace/MacGill Gallery, New York

**p. 30** Marcel Broodthaers, *White Cabinet and White Table*, 1965
Painted cabinet, table and eggshells, cabinet 86 x 82 x 62, table 104 x 100 x 40
Fractional and promised gift of Jo Carole and Ronald S. Lauder. © DACS 2012

**p. 31 left** Robert Ryman, *Classico 5*, 1968
Synthetic polymer paint on paper, overall 236.9 x 224.8
Purchased with funds provided by the Committee on Drawings, Richard S. Zeisler Bequest (by exchange), the estate of William S. Lieberman, The Edward John Noble Foundation, Kathy and Richard S. Fuld Jr, Marie-Josée and Henry R. Kravis, Marlene Hess and Jim Zirin, The Judith Rothschild Foundation, Sally and Wynn Kramarsky, Sharon Percy Rockefeller, and Aaron Fleischman. Photo John Wronn. © 2012 Robert Ryman / DACS, London

**p. 31 right** Piero Manzoni, *Achrome*, 1962
Fibreglass on velvet-covered wood, 81.3 x 64.8 x 26.4
Nina and Gordon Bunshaft Bequest, Mrs. John Hay Whitney Bequest, and Donald B. Marron Funds. © DACS 2012

**p. 32** Andreas Gursky, *Bahrain I*, 2005
Chromogenic colour print, 301.9 x 219.7
Acquired in honour of Robert B. Menschel through the generosity of Agnes Gund, Marie-Josée and Henry R. Kravis, Ronald S. and Jo Carole Lauder, and the Speyer Family Foundation. Photo Jonathan Muzikar. Courtesy Gallery Sprueth/Magers © DACS, London 2012

**p. 33** Gerhard Richter, *Flugzeug II (Airplane II)*, 1966
Screenprint, composition 48.6 x 81.4; sheet 61 x 86. Publisher Galerie Rottloff, Karlsruhe, Germany. Printer Löw Siebdruck, Stuttgart, Germany. Edition 20
Ann and Lee Fensterstock Fund, Alexandra Herzan Fund, and Virginia Cowles Schroth Fund. Photo David Allison. © Gerhard Richter 2012

**p. 34** Niki de Saint Phalle, *Shooting Painting American Embassy*, 1961
Paint, plaster, wood, plastic bags, shoe, twine, metal seat, axe, metal can, toy gun, wire mesh, bullet and other objects on wood, 244.8 x 65.7 x 21.9
Gift of the Niki Charitable Art Foundation. Photo John Wronn. © ADAGP, Paris and DACS, London 2012

**p. 35** Lucio Fontana, *Spatial Concept: Expectations*, 1960
Slashed canvas and gauze, 100.3 x 80.3
Gift of Philip Johnson. Photo Thomas Griesel. © Lucio Fontana / SIAE / DACS, London 2012

**p. 36** Martin Kippenberger, *Martin, Into the Corner, You Should Be Ashamed of Yourself*, 1992
Cast aluminium, clothing and iron plate, 181.6 x 74.9 x 34.3
Blanchette Hooker Rockefeller Fund Bequest, Anna Marie and Robert F. Shapiro, Jerry I. Speyer, and Michael and Judy Ovitz Funds. © Estate Martin Kippenberger, Galerie Gisela Capitain, Cologne

**p. 37 left** George Segal, *The Bus Driver*, 1962
Plaster over cheesecloth; bus parts including coin box, steering wheel, driver's seat, railing and dashboard, over wood and cinder blocks, overall 226 x 131 x 195
Philip Johnson Fund. © The George and Helen Segal Foundation / DACS, London / VAGA, New York 2012

**p. 37 right** Michelangelo Pistoletto, *Man with Yellow Pants*, 1964
Paper, oil and pencil on polished stainless steel, 200.3 x 100
Blanchette Hooker Rockefeller Fund. Photo Thomas Griesel. © Fondazione Pistoletto-Cittadellarte, Biella

**p. 38** Chris Ofili, *Prince Amongst Thieves*, 1999
Synthetic polymer paint, oil, paper collage, polyester glitter, resin, map pins and elephant dung on canvas, 243.8 x 182.9
Mimi and Peter Haas Fund. © Chris Ofili. Courtesy Victoria Miro Gallery, London. Photo Stephen White

**p. 39 left** Dieter Roth, *Basel on the Rhine*, 1969
Chocolate and steel, 80 x 80 x 4.6
Barbara Jakobson Fund and Jeanne C. Thayer Fund. © Dieter Roth Estate. Courtesy Hauser & Wirth

**p. 39 right** John Chamberlain, *Essex*, 1960
Automobile parts and other metal, 274.3 x 203.2 x 109.2
Gift of Mr and Mrs Robert C. Scull and purchase. Photo John Wronn. © ARS, NY and DACS, London 2012

**p. 40** Francis Alÿs, *Untitled*, 1994
Oil on canvas and synthetic polymer paint on sheet metal, three panels, small panel by Francis Alÿs 31.8 x 25.4, medium panel by Emilio Rivera 91.4 x 71.4, large panel by Juan Garcia 120 x 91.4
Gift of Eileen and Peter Norton. Courtesy David Zwirner, New York

**p. 41** Vija Celmins, *To Fix the Image in Memory*, 1977–82
Stones and painted bronze, eleven pairs, dimensions variable
Gift of Edward R. Broida in honour of David and Renee McKee. Photo Thomas Griesel. Courtesy McKee Gallery, New York

**p. 42** Barnett Newman, *Broken Obelisk*, 1963–69
Cor-Ten steel, 749.9 x 318.8 x 318.8
Given anonymously. Photo David Allison. © ARS, NY and DACS, London 2012

**p. 43 above** Peter Fischli and David Weiss, *The Way Things Go*, 1987
16mm film transferred to video, 31 minutes
Purchase. © Peter Fischli, David Weiss. Courtesy Matthew Marks Gallery, New York

**p. 43 below** Richard Serra, *One Ton Prop (House of Cards)*, 1969 (refabricated 1986)
Lead antimony, four plates, each 122 x 122 x 2.5
Gift of the Grinstein Family. © ARS, NY and DACS, London 2012

**p. 44** Do Ho Suh, *Doormat: Welcome*, 1998
Multiple of polyurethane rubber, 3.1 x 71.2 x 47.9. Edition 5
Robert and Anna Marie Shapiro Fund. Photo Peter Butler. © Do Ho Suh, 1998. Courtesy the artist and Lehmann Maupin Gallery, New York

**p. 45 above** Ed Ruscha, *OOF*, 1962 (reworked 1963)
Oil on canvas, 181.5 x 170.2
Gift of Agnes Gund, the Louis and Bessie Adler Foundation, Inc., Robert and Meryl Meltzer, Jerry I. Speyer, Anna Marie and Robert F. Shapiro, Emily and Jerry Spiegel, an anonymous donor, and purchase. Photo Thomas Griesel. © Ed Ruscha

**p. 45 below** Antoni Muntadas, *On Translation: Warning*, 1999–present

From a portfolio of twelve examples of ephemeral print projects including one newspaper, one poster, four stickers and six exhibition announcements, composition and sheet (each): various dimensions. Various publishers. Various editions
The Associates Fund. © Muntadas

**p. 46** Chris Burden, *Medusa's Head*, 1990
Plywood, steel, cement, rock, model railway trains and tracks, 426.7 diameter
Gift of Sid and Mercedes Bass. © Chris Burden. Courtesy Gagosian Gallery

**p. 47 left** Anna Maria Maiolino, *Buraco Preto (Black Hole)* from the series "Os Buracos/Desenhos Objetos" (Holes/Drawing Objects), 1974
Torn paper, 68.6 x 68.6
Purchase. © Anna Maria Maiolino

**p. 47 right** Lee Bontecou, *Untitled*, 1961
Welded steel, canvas, black fabric, rawhide, copper wire and soot, 203.6 x 226 x 88
Kay Sage Tanguy Fund. Photo Jonathan Muzikar. © 2012 Lee Bontecou

**p. 48** Donald Judd, *Untitled (Stack)*, 1967
Lacquer on galvanised iron, twelve units, each 22.9 x 101.6 x 78.7, installed vertically with 22.9 cm intervals
Helen Acheson Bequest (by exchange) and gift of Joseph Helman. © Judd Foundation. Licensed by VAGA, New York / DACS, London 2012

**p. 49** Andy Warhol, *Campbell's Soup Cans*, 1962
Synthetic polymer paint on thirty-two canvases, each canvas 50.8 x 40.6
Partial gift of Irving Blum. © The Andy Warhol Foundation for the Visual Arts / ARS, New York / DACS, London 2012

**p. 50** John Coplans, *Self Portrait*, 1985
Gelatin silver print, 33.4 x 42.9
Gift of Peter MacGill. © The John Coplans Trust

**p. 51** Janine Antoni, *Butterfly Kisses*, 1996–99
Cover Girl Thick Lash Mascara on paper, 75.6 x 76.2
Purchase. Photo John Wronn. Courtesy the artist and Luhring Augustine, New York

**p. 52** Jeff Koons, *Three Ball 50/50 Tank (Two Dr. J. Silver Series, One Wilson Supershot)*, 1985
Glass, painted steel, distilled water, plastic and three basketballs, 154 x 123.9 x 33.6
Gift of Werner and Elaine Dannheisser. Photo John Wronn. © Jeff Koons

**p. 53 above** Blinky Palermo, *Flipper*, 1970
Screenprint on two sheets, composition (each approx.) 80 x 60; sheet (each) 85 x 65.9. Publisher Galerie Heiner Friedrich, Munich / New York. Printer Atelier Laube, Munich. Edition 90
Walter Bareiss Fund and Sarah C. Epstein Fund. © DACS 2012

**p. 53 below** Gabriel Orozco, *Horses Running Endlessly*, 1995
Wood, 8.7 x 87.5 x 87.5
Gift of Agnes Gund and Lewis B. Cullman in honour of Chess in the Schools. © Gabriel Orozco. Courtesy Marian Goodman Gallery, New York

**p. 54** Rachel Whiteread, *Untitled (Mattress)*, 1991
Plaster, 30.5 x 188 x 137.2
Gift of Agnes Gund. Photo Thomas Griesel. © Rachel Whiteread

**p. 55** Louise Bourgeois, *Bed #1, state I*, 1997
Etching, drypoint and engraving with watercolour, ink and pencil additions, plate 41.6 x 50.2, sheet 51 x 58. Unpublished state. Printer Harlan & Weaver, New York. Early state before the edition of 100
Gift of the artist. © Louise Bourgeois Trust / DACS, London / VAGA, New York 2012

While every effort has been made to trace the copyright holders of the images contained in this book, in some cases this has not proved possible. The Publisher welcomes hearing from any copyright holders who have not been notified and would be pleased to insert the appropriate acknowledgment in any subsequent edition of this book.

# INDEX

Page numbers in **bold** refer to illustrations

## A

Abstract Expressionist 13
Acconci, Vito 27, **27**
Alÿs, Francis **2–3**, 40, **40**
Antoni, Janine 51, **51**
assemblage 34
Azúa, Martín 23, **23**

## B

Beuys, Joseph 26, **26**
Bontecou, Lee 47, **47**
Bourgeois, Louise 55, **55**
Broodthaers, Marcel 30, **30**
Burden, Chris **46**, 47
Buren, Daniel 25, **25**
Byars, James Lee 22, **22**

## C

Cage, John 15
Celmins, Vija 41, **41**
Chamberlain, John **4**, 39, **39**
Chillida, Eduardo 25, **25**
Close, Chuck 17, **17**
collages 20
colour 7, 8–9, 10, 13, 19, 24, 30, 31, 33, 53
    black 25, 33, 47, 50, 53
    blue 8, 9, 10, 53
    gold, 22–23
    green 9, 10, 33, 48
    grey 14, 25
    orange 9
    pink 10, 33
    red 9, 10, 53
    silver 23
    ultraviolet 10
    violet 9
    white 10, 14, 25, 30–31, 53
    yellow 10
conceptual artist 40
Coplans, John 50, **50**

## D

drawing 6, 25, 49, 51

## E

Eliasson, Olafur 9, **9**

## F

film 26, 43
Fischli, Peter and Weiss, David 43, **43**
Flavin, Dan 10, **10**
Fontana, Lucio 35, **35**
Fontcuberta, Joan 21, **21**
Formiguera, Pere 21, **21**

## G

Gonzales-Torres, Felix 29, **29**
Gursky, Andreas **32**, 33

## H

Hirst, Damien **5**, 19, **19**

## I

installation 6, 27, 40, 45, 48

## J

Judd, Donald 48, **48**

## K

Kippenberger, Martin 36, **36**
Klein, Yves 8, **8**
Koons, Jeff 52, **52**

## L

Lampert, Nicolas 20, **20**
Lichtenstein, Roy 13, **13**
Long, Richard 18, **18**, 19
Louis, Morris 24, **24**

## M

Maiolino, Anna Maria 47, **47**
Manzoni, Piero 31, **31**
Martin, Agnes 23, **23**
materials 28, 39, 43, 47
    aluminium 36
    asphalt 33
    balloons 43
    bandages 37
    basketballs 52
    bread rolls 31
    bronze 6, 41
    bus seats 37
    cabinets 30
    candles 43
    canvas 13, 14, 24, 27, 31, 35, 47
    cardboard 33
    cars 6, 39

[*materials cont.*]
    cement 47
    cheese 39
    chocolate 6, 39
    clay 31
    clocks 29
    cloth 25, 28
    conveyor belts 47
    cotton padding 31
    crayon 14
    cups 43
    eggs/eggshells 7, 30, 39
    elephant dung 6, 39
    fat 26
    felt 15, 26
    fibreglass wool 31
    footprints 18
    furniture 30
    fuse wire 43
    glitter 39
    gold 22–23
    gold leaf 22, 23
    granite 25
    ink 6, 19, 33
    iron 25
    jeans 36
    ladders 43
    lead 43
    leather 47
    light 7, 10–11, 27
    lightbulbs 10, 19, 39
    magazine cutouts 39
    map pins 39
    marble 6, 22
    mascara 51
    masking tape 31
    mattresses 43
    metal plates 43
    metal seats 34
    mirrors 37
    model railway trains 39, 47
    neon 11
    oil drums 43
    paint 6, 8, 13, 14, 31, 34, 51
    paper 8, 19, 25, 31, 47, 51
    park benches 37
    pianos 15
    pine needles 18
    plaster 28, 37, 54
    rabbit skin 31
    ramps 43
    resin 54
    rocks 47
    rubber 44, 54

[*materials cont.*]
    scrap metal 39
    seesaws 43
    shirts 36
    shoes 34, 36
    slate 18
    soot 47
    steel 15, 25, 28, 39, 42, 47
    stickers 45
    stones 18, 41
    street signs 37
    suits 26
    tables 30
    television screens 15
    toy guns 34
    tyres 43
    watercolours 49
    wood 18, 25
Minimalist artist 48
Morris, Robert 15, **15**
multimedia artist 45
Muntadas, Antoni 45, **45**

## N

Nauman, Bruce 11, **11**
Newman, Barnett 42, **42**

## O

Ofili, Chris **38**, 39
Oldenburg, Claes 28, **28**
Op art 13
Orozco, Gabriel 53, **53**

## P

Paik, Nam June 15, **15**
painting 6, 13, 14, 17, 19, 23, 24, 25, 30, 34, 35, 37, 39, 40, 45, 48, 49
Palermo, Blinky 53, **53**
pattern 33, 41, 53
performance 6, 8, 34, 51
photography 6, 17, 18, 20, 21, 26, 29, 33, 45, 50
Pistoletto, Michelangelo 37, **37**
Pollock, Jackson **12**, 13
Pop artist 28
print 9, 19, 33, 49, 53, 55

## R

Richter, Gerhard 33, **33**
Riley, Bridget 13, **13**
Ross, Judith Joy 29, **29**
Roth, Dieter 39, **39**
Ruscha, Ed 45, **45**
Ryman, Robert 31, **31**

## S

Saint Phalle, Niki de 34, **34**
screenprint 33
sculpture 6, 10, 15, 18, 19, 25, 28, 30, 35, 36, 37, 39, 42, 43, 47, 48, 54
Segal, George 37, **37**
Serra, Richard 43, **43**
shape 7, 8, 10, 11, 15, 18, 33, 48
    boxes 48
    circles 17, 18–19, 47
    crosses 18
    cubes 22, 48
    grids 23, 31
    lines 7, 13, 18, 19, 23, 24–25, 31
    ovals 17
    rectangles 31, 48
    spirals 18
    stripes 25
    triangles 17
studio 19, 24
studio assistant 14
Suh, Do Ho 44, **44**
Surrealist art 30

## T

Tanaka, Atsuko **1**, 19, **19**
techniques/tools
    blades 35
    brushes 13, 25
    cast/casting 36, 41, 54
    eyelashes 51
    fabric screen 33
    knives 13
    "living paintbrushes" 8
    needles 19
    rollers 8
    screwdrivers 19
    sponges 8
    stencils 33
    trowels 13
Twombly, Cy 14, **14**

## U

urban interventions 45

## V

video art 6, 15, 45

## W

Warhol, Andy 49, **49**
Wearing, Gillian **16**, 17
Whiteread, Rachel 54, **54**

For Clara, Louis, Joe, Harry
and the next generation of art lovers

## ABOUT THE AUTHORS

Jacky Klein studied at Oxford University and the Courtauld Institute of Art, London. Formerly a curator at the Hayward Gallery and an assistant curator at Tate Modern, she is the author of *Grayson Perry* (Thames & Hudson, 2009). She works in publishing and lives in London.

Suzy Klein studied at Oxford University and City University, London. She writes and broadcasts on the arts and culture, presenting widely on BBC television and radio, and is a contributor to the *Guardian* newspaper and *New Statesman* magazine. She lives in London with her husband and two children.

## ACKNOWLEDGMENTS

Our thanks go to Christopher Hudson, Kara Kirk and the publications, education and curatorial departments at The Museum of Modern Art, New York, for their guidance, knowledge and collaborative spirit throughout; to Jamie Camplin at Thames & Hudson for his original thinking in conceiving this book; to the dedicated and hardworking team at Thames & Hudson who have so beautifully realised this book; to the picture researcher, Jo Walton; to Gilda Williams, whose early ideas played a part in the shaping of this project; to Mary Jordan, Head of Art, and the grade four children of Mr Kish's 2011 art class at the American School, London, for their enthusiasm and thoughtful insights; and to Theo for his razor-sharp editorial skills and endless supply of age-appropriate adjectives. Finally, our enduring love and thanks to Mum, Dad, James and Granny P for their unstinting encouragement, support and babysitting.

Front cover: Claes Oldenburg, *Two Cheeseburgers, with Everything (Dual Hamburgers)*, 1962
Burlap soaked in plaster, painted with enamel, 17.8 x 37.5 x 21.8 cm. The Museum of Modern Art, New York. Philip Johnson Fund. Courtesy the Oldenburg van Bruggen Studio. © 1962 Claes Oldenburg

Endpapers: Janine Antoni, *Butterfly Kisses*, 1996–99 [detail]
Cover Girl Thick Lash Mascara on paper, 75.6 x 76.2 cm The Museum of Modern Art, New York. Purchase. Photo John Wronn. Courtesy the artist and Luhring Augustine, New York

First published in the United Kingdom in 2012 by Thames & Hudson Ltd, 181A High Holborn, London WC1V 7QX
Copyright © 2012 Jacky Klein and Suzy Klein

British Library Cataloguing-in-Publication Data
A catalogue record for this book is available from the British Library

ISBN 978-0-500-51589-1

Printed and bound in China through Asia Pacific Offset Ltd

To find out about all our publications, please visit **www.thamesandhudson.com**. There you can subscribe to our e-newsletter, browse or download our current catalogue, and buy any titles that are in print.